OUR FAVORITE DOG MEMORIES

FINDING COMFORT THROUGH COLORING TOGETHER

BY CLAY HORTON

Copyright © 2024 by Clay Horton
ISBN: 9798324555320

Cover Illustration by Brenna Horton
The quotes provided in the book are not attributed to specific individuals. They are general sentiments expressing the relationship between dogs and kids.

A NOTE TO PARENTS & ADULTS

Saying goodbye to our family dog was one of the toughest days of my life. Emotionally, I knew the day was coming. We made sure to make it a great morning. I gave him an egg and some cheese, and my wife and I tried to make it the best car ride ever. I won't recount the time at the vet, but our vet made it a peaceful and beautiful goodbye. We shed tears and we drove home with empty hearts in our empty car.

But then it hit us. It was now time to face the kids who had joyfully and obliviously spent a great morning with their grandparents. What would we tell the kids? How would we tell the kids?

Losing an animal is oftentimes one of the first times children experience grief. All the family members find themselves grieving, often at different stages of grief. It's important for the children to see adults in their lives grieve in a healthy way. From tears, to sharing fun memories, to lots of hugs, the loss of a dog is a milestone in one's life and the children will learn to grieve by watching the adults.

In the midst of our grieving, some good friends dropped off a care package. Along with Scoobie Snacks for the kids and a bottle of wine with a dog on it for the adults, they gave us some crayons and a giant roll of butcher paper. As we unrolled the paper, we discovered drawing prompts to help us remember our dog. As we colored together, each drawing our own pet memory for each prompt, our hearts were united in grief and the celebration of a great dog. It was perhaps the single "best" experience for us during that time.

After that experience, we've tried to do something similar for other friends who say goodbye to their pets. But, shipping a giant roll of butcher paper in the mail is a little too complicated. This book is hopefully the next best thing. It is written to help you and your family move through the grieving process together. My heart goes out to you and my hope is that this book will help capture the memories you shared with your dog while also creating a new memory for your family.

KIDS AND DOGS GO
TOGETHER LIKE PEANUT
BUTTER AND JELLY.

HOW TO USE THIS BOOK

This book is designed to help you remember and celebrate your dog. In fact, your dog is the star of the book! Each page is an opportunity to draw a memory about your dog.

Each person can take turns drawing in the book. You can choose to have one person draw per page, or have multiple people in your family draw a picture on each page. It's certainly ok for each person to have their own thoughts and ideas about your dog's favorite things!

Some of the pages will make you laugh and some might even make you cry. Remember that the people who you are reading with, love you and loved your dog. It's perfectly OK to feel all the emotions and it can be very healing to feel these emotions together. Use this book to create an experience to share memories together.

KIDS AND DOGS: A MATCH MADE IN HEAVEN.

THIS BOOK IS ALL ABOUT...
(DRAW A PICTURE OF YOUR AWESOME DOG!)

A CHILD'S FAVORITE GAME: 'LET'S SEE HOW MANY TOYS WE CAN FIT IN THE DOG'S MOUTH!'

MY DOG'S FAVORITE TOY

GROWING UP WITH A DOG IS LIKE HAVING A FURRY SIBLING.

MY DOG'S FAVORITE SLEEPING POSITION

DOGS AND KIDS: PARTNERS IN MISCHIEF, ALLIES IN FUN.

THE FARTHEST MY DOG TRAVELED FROM HOME

A DOG'S LOVE KNOWS NO BOUNDS, ESPECIALLY WHEN IT COMES TO KIDS.

MY DOG'S
FAVORITE FOOD

A DOG'S TAIL IS THE BEST METRONOME FOR A CHILD'S LAUGHTER.

MY DOG TAKING
A CAR RIDE

DOGS ARE THE PERFECT PLAYMATES FOR CHILDHOOD ADVENTURES.

MY DOG GREETING ME WHEN I GOT HOME

EVERY CHILD NEEDS A DOG TO GROW UP WITH, AND
EVERY DOG NEEDS A CHILD TO LOVE.

MY DOG'S FAVORITE
THING TO DO

DOGS TEACH KIDS ABOUT RESPONSIBILITY AND
EMPATHY WITHOUT SAYING A WORD.

THIS IS WHAT MY DOG
LOOKED LIKE BEFORE AND
AFTER A HAIRCUT OR BATH

A CHILD'S LAUGHTER IS THE MUSIC THAT MAKES A DOG'S TAIL WAG.

MY DOG'S FAVORITE PLACE IN THE HOUSE

DOGS HAVE A MAGICAL WAY OF TURNING ORDINARY MOMENTS INTO UNFORGETTABLE MEMORIES FOR KIDS.

THESE ARE MY DOG'S NICKNAMES

IN THE EYES OF A CHILD, A DOG IS A HERO WITHOUT A CAPE.

MY DOG'S FAVORITE PLACE TO BE SCRATCHED

KIDS AND DOGS: THE ULTIMATE TAG TEAM FOR LEAVING
SURPRISES ON THE LIVING ROOM FLOOR.

THIS IS THE GROSSEST THING MY DOG EVER DID!

A DOG'S LOVE IS THE SECRET INGREDIENT THAT MAKES
CHILDHOOD UNFORGETTABLE.

MY DOG'S FAVORITE PLACE TO GO

DOGS TEACH KIDS THAT LOVE COMES IN ALL
SHAPES, SIZES, AND FUR COLORS.

THIS IS WHAT I WILL REMEMBER THE MOST ABOUT MY DOG

10 MORE WAYS TO REMEMBER

1. Create a Memory Collage: Gather photos, drawings, and mementos of your dog to create a beautiful collage that captures their spirit and the special moments you shared together.

2. Plant a Memorial Garden: Select a spot in your yard or a community garden to plant flowers, herbs, or a tree in memory of your dog.

3. Talk it Out: Create an appointment for your child to talk with a counselor or children's minister.

4. Hold a Memorial Service: Invite family and friends to gather. Share memories, light candles, or blow bubbles as a sign of letting go.

5. Re-Read this Memory Book: Flip through the pages of this book whenever you want to feel close to them. Leave this book out in an easy to see place so that you'll be able to flip through it often.

6. Donate to Animal Charities: Honor your dog's memory by donating to animal shelters, rescue organizations, or other charities that support furry friends in need. Helping other animals in their name can be a meaningful way to celebrate their legacy.

7. Create a Special Keepsake: Craft a personalized keepsake such as a clay paw print, a custom ornament, or a memorial plaque engraved with your dog's name and dates. These tangible reminders can provide comfort and solace during difficult times.

8. Visit Their Favorite Places: Take a trip to your dog's favorite park, beach, or hiking trail to honor their adventurous spirit and love for the great outdoors. Spend time in the places where you made cherished memories together.

9. Create a Memory Jar: Set up a memory jar in your home where family members can write down their favorite memories, funny anecdotes, or heartfelt messages about your dog. At the end of each week or month, gather together to read and reminisce about the moments that brought joy to your lives.

10. Start a Tradition: Establish a special tradition or ritual to honor your dog's memory on meaningful occasions such as their birthday, the anniversary of their passing, or holidays. Whether it's lighting a candle, sharing a favorite treat, or taking a moment of silence, these rituals can provide comfort and connection as you remember your dog.

Did your family find this book helpful? If so, please leave a review on Amazon so that other families can find this resource as well.

Scan to leave a review or purchase a copy to give to a friend.

Made in the USA
Las Vegas, NV
24 September 2024